Dialogue
a Mind and
a Heart

By
Paola Zanoni

MAPLE
PUBLISHERS

Dialogues Between a Mind and a Heart

Author: Paola Zanoni

Copyright © 2024 Paola Zanoni

The right of Paola Zanoni to be identified as author of this work has been asserted by the author in accordance with section 77 and 78 of the Copyright, Designs and Patents Act 1988.

First Published in 2024

ISBN 978-1-83538-306-3 (Paperback)
      978-1-83538-998-0 (Hardback)
      978-1-83538-307-0 (E-Book)

Book Cover Design and Book Layout by:
      White Magic Studios
      www.whitemagicstudios.co.uk

Published by:
      Maple Publishers
      Fairbourne Drive, Atterbury,
      Milton Keynes,
      MK10 9RG, UK
      www.maplepublishers.com

To My Younger Self,

Once when I was a 10 years old I asked myself – Do I need to follow my Heart or my Mind? This question bothered me all my life; as an adult I have found my answer and is that people should think with their hearts and feel with their minds, so they would think with love and they would love wisely - This book is a parabola of life where Heart and Mind share dialogues to understand each other better -

Table Of Content

THE ENCOUNTER

Once upon a time there was a Heart and a Mind that met by chance, in a park of the large city. It was Sunday morning and Heart decided to go for a walk to the park called Hope, near his house. That morning, like every Sunday, Heart put on his best clothes. He felt happy and the sun, on the warm morning of May, shone brighter than ever. When he arrived at the park Heart began to contemplate its beauty. "How beautiful" said Heart "I love the flowers, I love the plants and the swans on the pond and the sun that shines in the sky".

The Park Hope was located in the center of the city called Cityland. It was a park in the shape of a circle, like the floor plan of the earth; at the two poles there were two small ponds with swans and ducks, in the north and red fishes, like Japanese style gardens, in the south. In the middle of the park was a tree that was at least a hundred years old that made the park very majestic. All around, it was surrounded by flowers (lilies, violets, roses and tulips) of a thousand colors and shapes that gave to the park a relaxing atmosphere and a unique scent. The park was surrounded by a footpath and many footpath branches within it, to allow pedestrians to walk through the park. Near the south pond there was a fruit plant, the only one in the whole park, a red apple plant.

That morning, Mind also decided to go for a walk to Hope Park. Mind was a very logical and serious individual: "I will go to the park from 10am to 12am he said to himself!!"

Mind, always very elegant, he left the house and headed to the park. When he arrived at the park, Mind thought "everything is so beautiful, the flowers with their wonderful colors that are shining under the beautiful warm sun of the day, and the swans, and the trees". It was a beautiful day.

Heart sat on a bench full of love and serenity.

Mind sat on a bench contemplating the beauty of the park.

Heart saw Mind; Mind was on the bench next to him he smiled at Heart and looked at him with curiosity.

Suddenly, a big dark cloud obscured the sky, and within minutes thunder, lightning, and rain covered the park.

Heart got up and started to jump, "how beautiful, how beautiful" he shouted out loud.

Mind, who was always well prepared, opened his umbrella. He looked at Heart, intrigued and surprised, and asked "Why are you so happy?"

"Because I love the rain," answered Heart.

Mind not understanding said "but you get wet, and the rain is unpleasant, and I find it annoying, it puts me in a bad mood" added Mind.

Heart looked at Mind not understanding what he was referring to and kept jumping and dancing under the rain.

"What's your name?" said Mind more and more curious

"I am Heart, and what's your name?"

"I am Mind, please to meet you," Mind told Heart, who never stopped jumping and singing.

"What makes you so happy? What do you love?" asked Mind,

"The beauty of life, life itself," Heart replied.

Mind didn't understand and said, "but life is hard, it's tiring and tormented and full of problems and worries".

At this point Heart stopped dancing, he looked at Mind perplexed…. The two looked each other in the eyes.

"What do you want from life," Mind asked Heart.

"To love" said heart full of himself, " and what do you want from life, Mind?"

"TO GET TO KNOW YOU!!!!"

HEARTY

"How do you achieve love?" asked Mind with an inquisitive thought.

"I was once a lonely Heart," Heart said, "Loneliness takes you and does not leave you, it haunts you. My loneliness was based on the fact that I thought I needed another Heart to suppress it. When I was a kid, I lived in the desert with my Dad and my brothers and sisters. My mum died when I was just a newborn. Growing up, my world was no longer enough for me; I wanted more! Later on I moved to this big city. At first it was very hard, I was even more alone, not only emotionally but also physically. I started to make new acquaintances but I also felt alone in the middle of people. Until one day in this park I met my other half..... another Heart"

"Hello!" said Hearty "Are you passing by?"

"No, I moved here a while ago." I replied.

"Where are you from?" she asked me softly.

"I'm from the south," I replied, "from a village called Burning"

"Ah! I went there once, it's an unforgettable place," said Hearty, stroking her hair with grace.

"And so our friendship began and we fell in love. When we saw each other, everything was magical. We spent days together, and my loneliness started to fade away slowly."

"We spent our afternoons in this park, looking at the swans, we walked hand by hand through the park, talked about our dreams, our hopes and the beauties of the world."

"Those were very beautiful moments!" admitted Heart. "Right in this park, there is a small cave and it is said that when two Hearts are in tune a coloured butterfly flies out from the cave. The caterpillar turns into a butterfly spreading love around the park."

"This park is very magical, you know," said Heart, "Every little thing has its own peculiarity, from ants that carry a small leaf to their anthill, to bees pollinating flowers; to the grasshoppers that jump in tune with the wind; and the musicality of birdsong. And this was our love and world for a while."

"So the key to love is having a partner," Mind said.

Heart got serious and looking at Mind in the eyes said, "Having a companion can soften loneliness for a little while but it is not the key to learn how to love; it takes much deeper understanding." Heart carried on and said, "I was young and immature at the time, and I felt that I wanted my freedom, so after a while our first conflicts began. I felt strong feelings towards her but I was in conflict with myself because I wanted to make my dreams come true; I wanted to be free and I was afraid of this strong commitment between us. I did not want to take this relationship too seriously but I did not want to leave her either. So she started to suffer and our first problems as a couple began. In those days I was a young man full of energy and very eager to accomplish myself in this world," said Heart "but I felt there was something missing; I was looking for something that I already had and I did not know how to value it."

"Our story soon after ended. We decided to go our separate ways. It wasn't an easy decision, it took a lot of strength and it was very painful."

Soon after, Hearty moved to another country due to her work. Before she left, she gave me a keyring of the shape of love, and she said to me "go and find the key to your heart."

I suffered a lot and missed her very much but I understood something important; and this was that I was in conflict with myself.

At that exact moment began my long journey for the search of pure love. I understood that dreams can come true but it is love that leads us to the right path; although we may encounter difficulties and stumble or take a few steps back or worse stop in time; despite all these, dreams can come true if one really is willing to believe in themselves and in their own wishes and also learns to let it go.

Mind listened to the story with great interest and asked Heart, "What is the shape of love?"

Then Heart with a shy smile said "The shape of love is unique for each individual but the intrinsic meaning is the same for everyone".

THE MAGICIAN

The next day Heart returned to the park carefree and with a serious attitude. There it was Mind busy reading the newspaper of the day. Heart approached him and asked "then, is it good news," Mind replied to him all thoughtfully, "it's sad the bad things that happen in the world and you talk about love." And the two started a lively debate about the misfortunes that were happening in the world.

Heart understood that Mind was a pretty stubborn guy, and that when he had a point of view on something, he didn't let it go easily. Heart silently laughed because he realized Mind was looking for something but he didn't know himself what it was.

"I'll tell you something," Heart said, "you want to know me better and I will tell you facts that left an imprint in my life during my search for love" Heart carried on, "when my Hearty left, I was confused and lost. Nothing mattered to me and I felt more alone than ever; She gave me a task and it was to find the key to my heart. This gave me a lot of strength to face this separation from her."

Heart carried on and sat near Mind, took the newspaper from his hands and placed it on the bench "How do you achieve such a goal?" I asked myself.

"I began to wander like a nomad around the city with my keyring in my pocket; I looked at people and they seemed alone, immersed in their world; there were those who seemed more optimistic but there were people who seemed frightened; there were people who seemed very busy and who had no time to spare to look around, and there were people walking around lost, they seemed to have no goal in life" Heart took a breath "I understood that I was not alone;" and he carried on "I had a mission, I had promised my Hearty that I would accomplish it!"

Heart stood up and asked Mind if he would fancy a walk. Mind agreed, and the two headed to the center of the park. "One day you know I met a magician, yes really! a magician" He was in the main street of the city, he was performing some magic tricks. When the show was over, we started talking; I told him about my problem and that I was looking for a key that was the key to my heart.

Then the magician picked up his hat and took a white handkerchief. So he made a move as the magicians usually do in their acts of magic. From the hat came out a dove with a pink key in his mouth and it flew away.

I was stunned, I got angry at him!!! But how could he let the dove go away with the key; "How could you do that!!!" I cried with a red face full of rage and then desperate with tears in my eyes, I said, "How could you?". The magician laughed, he was a funny person dressed in black with two long mustaches, bold, and wore a hat at least thirty centimeters high. He said to me "what you saw is an illusion, what you are looking for you have to find it inside you!!" "But where did the dove go?" I shouted! He replied, "To your beloved."

THE LETTING GO

I was shocked; I didn't understand... how could I find the answers inside me if my key had flown away? I felt hopeless, astonished, angry!!!

Mind always with this intellectual and refined approach said "I do not understand where you want to go from here: love, happiness are only small components of our lives. Real life is money, work, effort and trying to alleviate the suffering to which we are put through every day. You tell me about love that leads to happiness but that it's not real life, that's living in a dream!"

Then Heart shyly asked "Have you ever had a dream Mind? What do you dream about?"

Mind a little tired from the walk, stopped and adjusted his jacket, put himself in a straight position and replied "I have dreamed many times but my dreams have crumbled like sand castles over the years. When I was young I wanted to achieve success, to be important, I wanted to become an artist. Unfortunately life circumstances have led me on different paths. At times in life, one makes choices and you lose focus from your dreams; sometimes you make decisions driven by a little bit of laziness, sometimes a little bit because you think it's the only solution at that time; sometimes on that moment, you believe your choice it's a good idea; but then as you get older you realize you've lived but you haven't achieved your life fulfillment, your dreams."

Heart smiled and said "life is all a point of view my dear Mind! It's not what you do, but how you do it... the hard thing is to put it into practice." "And I'll explain why."

"After getting upset by the dove flying away with the key, I immediately called my Hearty and asked if she had seen the dove. She replied that she had received the key and then she asked me, "Have you found yours?" Then more confused than ever I got angry at her and said "how can you commission me such an impossible task. Where can I find it and how and why?" I was hurt, angry, I felt a victim in a conflict of emotions, I was confused and I couldn't figure out a way out.

The next day I meditated about the whole situation and I decided to let go of that nonsense and unrealistic mission. After all, it only gave me pain and confusion.

I decided to focus on myself, as you did Mind, to accomplish what I thought were my dreams and I abandoned completely the idea of the search for love.

THE WISE MAN

My dream was to become an accomplished musician but I went in all other directions. I was spending lots of time on my own playing music to alleviate the pain inside me; the emptiness I had inside was being comforted by the music I was playing. My songs were about a search, my separation from my Hearty and the cruelty of life. I devoted myself to a mundane way of life; I went out every night, drank the impossible, took drugs, threw myself into the hands of many women with the intention of finding comfort in my loneliness and the emptiness I felt inside.

However, I always carried my keyring in my pocket, hoping to find that key that would lead to love and happiness. Things got worse and I began to see no more future in front of me, no more a way out. I was at home composing music, I drank and cried because I felt lost. I felt like I was in a boat in the middle of the sea in the middle of a shipwreck, not being able to see a place to land. In addition there was a desire in me for self-destruction.

One day, after I drank a bottle of whisky, I went around Cityland; that town seemed more familiar to me but everything was detached from me. I started hallucinating from all the drugs and alcohol I have taken; people were looking at me, talking about me, I was panicking and that day almost miraculously I had a strange encounter.

I met a man dressed in white who said to me; "are you alright? Looking for something?" Then I said abruptly "I am ok, I just want to be left alone" but he didn't give up.

He was a tall man, with fair hair and a long beard, he had a stick in his hand and unexpectedly said to me "What you are looking for you will find it; but you must not use only your instincts, you have to use your heart"

"But what are you talking about," I said in shock!

"You know what I mean" he said with a smile on his face; I noticed at this point the serene expression of his face showing kindness and understanding, while he swapped the stick in the other hand, he said "you are looking for answers"

"Yes," I admitted.

"What exactly are you looking for?" asked the man dressed in white

"A key." I replied.

"Why are you looking for a key?" he said with a calm voice.

"Because I want to understand love and happiness."

"What's happiness for you?"

"A state of mind that is unknown to me and far away from me." I replied to him with a feeling of sadness.

"Where do you think you're going to find this key you are looking for?" he asked me with a supportive and compassionate look.

"Why are you looking at me like that?" I shouted angrily at him!! and I added "Happiness is out there somewhere!"

And the mysterious man said, "And you feel like you're going to find happiness and love, hmm out there?" and the mysterious man made a noise with his throat almost with the intention of starting a fairly serious speech but then he said , "So.....let's summarize; do you think that love is the key to happiness and do you think you will find it in the outside world, right?"

"Yes," I replied reassured.

"But then tell me," said the man, "where did you look for it in drugs, in alcohol, in mundane life?"

"That was my way out," I replied!!

"So you're looking for the key that brings you happiness but at the same time you fear it and you escape from it."

"I don't understand, " I said, intrigued and mad because I felt I was wasting my time making nonsense speeches with a stranger!!

"Then you think the key is out there and you have to go and get it; at the same time you don't know how to get there; you don't have the means, you don't know the way. So I tell you today is your lucky day." he said, and I looked at him even more intrigue. The man opened the top of the stick and took a key that had a strange shape. It was made of ivory on the outside and the inside was made of solid wood.

"Here for you is the key you've been looking for; now you have it and make good use of it."

"But who are you?" I asked astonished "your guardian angel,"" he replied.

I looked at the key and took it and when I looked up the man was gone. I turned my head left and right, turned the corner of the street but he had disappeared completely. And I stood with the key in my hand stunned and confused.

"Now I'm starting to understand," Mind said, and he added "Hey, who was that man?"

Heart said, "It doesn't matter who he was, what matters is what he made me understand: if you want something, you have to go and get it, don't run away or escape from it"

"What happened from that moment on, since you found your key?" Asked Mind with a skeptical attitude but this time with a glimmer of light in his face. Heart noticed it and was very pleased.

"My life changed completely, not because I had the key but because I understood the meaning of my search".

Mind looked at the clock and said with a hasty attitude "I don't have time to listen to these talks; I have a lot of things to do at the moment, I'm a committed and a very dedicated person! "

Heart laughed and Mind added "These are all nonsense, life is made of sacrifices and responsibility, not nonsense search for love and keys, keyring and happiness... these are all idealistic speeches for dreamers and irresponsible people!"

Mind adjusted his hair, lit a cigar, warmly saluted Heart (Mind knew good manners very well!) and went away with his nose up, trying to show a disinterested attitude, with his umbrella in his hand (Mind was always well equipped) and he started walking towards the exit of the park.

Heart laughed and said to him "Tomorrow, same place, same time?"

Then Mind prouder than ever said "I have more important things to do than listen to the fantasies of a Heart in search of the absurd."

Heart smiled and said, "see you tomorrow then."

THE BOOK OF POEMS

The next day Heart noticed that Mind had already arrived and that he was sitting at the usual bench and noticed that he was also early. He had an expression of thoughtfulness. "Mind knew how to appreciate the beauty around him," Heart admitted. Mind noticed Heart, but he pretended not to see him.

"Good morning!" Heart said;

Heart noticed that Mind was not reading the newspaper with the usual catastrophic news, but he had a book in his hand.

Heart said "I see you're reading a book." he asked "What is this book about Mind?"

"I am very busy at the moment, I wish I would not be disturbed please."

But with a perplexed face Mind explained "This book is a book of poems, where people express all their sufferings in the name of love, of betrayals, of broken hearted and corrupted love. These are poems that tell the truth about love and happiness. "

"And what would be that truth that these people are talking about?" asked Heart "that love is suffering and pain that people do not even know what it is because too many tears have been cried in the name of love and many more people have suffered, this is the pure and only truth"

Heart answered with a smile on his face "Mind, you don't have to understand love, you need to feel it!"

Mind closed the book and explained his doubts to Heart and with a loud voice he said "Oh Heart, Heart" said Mind "you are telling me so many anecdotes and stories, although I struggle to believe you" and he added "Oh my Heart, how much suffering you had to go through, endure, face in your life in the name of love?" He stood up and raised the tone of the voice even more and said "Oh Heart! That love of which you speak seems a treasure to be found but why people are so unhappy, why they hurt each other to gain power and not the wisdom that only good can bring. Only a few like the great Socrates said "I know that I know nothing"; instead people are so self-centered and selfish especially between each other ""where is the world going oh Heart. Where's that treasure you're talking about?"

Mind took a flower in his hand and began to whisper "Oh Heart, Heart do you think that with a flower you can solve the dilemma of the heart. She loves me, she loves me not; the truth is that if you don't love yourself, you can't force others to love you, and you can't love someone you're not attracted to. What do you see in that flower?" Mind added, "How many petals it has, and when you are left in your hands with the center, with the essence of the flower, what do you do with it? What do you do with that flower that made you dream for a while? You throw it away as people throw away their dreams? In the name of what? They don't even know themselves! And so they pick up another flower and they start all over again without knowing what to do next, what way to go." and after a moment of silence Mind said "Oh Heart, you that understand the center of that flower, that yellow center like the sun, help me to reach, to find that love that you so much talk about, because I feel confused in this world, I feel lost. In life we have so many choices and responsibilities, I just want to understand, and being understood."

Mind then sat down, took a flower in his hand and added "Oh Heart what is the center of this flower for you? Tell me Heart; When is the time to abandon a dream and build new ones? When should we surrender to our fate? Is this right or wrong?; Oh Heart, Heart!!! Save me from this loneliness, from this struggling search, and teach me peace!"

THE SEARCH IS OVER

"You know Heart, I don't believe in love because my wife left me for another man, three years after we were married. My son was only one year old. From that moment I thought that life was cruel. I am telling you this because I want you to realize that it is not possible to be just a dreamer, we must be realistic in this world."

"My dear friend Mind, the world is a perception, life experiences are challenges, and life is very but very precious, but if you do not respect it, then it becomes an nightmare, and not only yours, but also for our loved ones, and the people we meet every day in our life path."

"With this," Heart added, "I want to tell you that sufferings are there and we must take them as teachings lessons and as constructive obstacles; and when you have overcome one, you then realized how good life is; you have learned from that lessons and you must be ready for the next battle; life is made of attempts, and the important thing is not to be afraid but to experience life, because - Life doesn't end here, but it's in a constant evolution!"

"Keeping this in mind, I will give you my key now, search for the door to open your heart, that lock that will allow you to understand and see. I suggest that this should not be an obsessive search but a wise search. I found my inner peace in this park, in this city, in the memories of the past and in the creation of the future, but above all in the expression of the present."

Heart carried on and said "I haven't finished telling you the story between me and my Hearty. I never stopped loving her and a few years later she contacted me and we met in this park." As soon as she saw me she said, "Hello my Heart!!" and she added, "do you want to spend a lifetime with me now that we both have the key? Now we just have to open that door to our hearts and open ourselves to love."

I nodded and added "I love you and we just have to live this love."

"I love you My Heart," she said.

"I love you Hearty," I said, "let's go open that door that will take us to a whole new level of life!! A life where everything is possible and unpredictable, where we will grow together and get older together, always and exclusively in search of a space of happiness, and above all of harmony and serenity with ourselves and with the outer world, always united!"

Mind took the key and said to heart, "I'm going to try to find that lock that's going to open the door to my heart. Thank you Heart for this gift!!"

"Remember Mind," Heart said, "that you must be in tune with your heart so that you can feel happiness. Every heart is bound to their mind and every mind is bound to their heart. Only when they are in tune the soul is in peace. For this, I tell you that, you have to find that lock that will open your heart and allow yourself to live peacefully, despite the ups and downs of life; the important thing is to be in tune with your own heart and your own mind; it is an achievable goal, if you are wise and you understand on how and where to look for. It's not an easy task because things don't always go as we'd like and life itself is unpredictable. But the secret of serenity is the harmony between our own heart and our own mind. In this dream that we are living in, the important thing is to find love and believe in it without doubts. It is important to be in tune with your body, with your thoughts, illusions and dreams. Do not despair that the finish line is near if you are determined to lead a wise life in the name of justice and truth.

Mind got up from the bench and with the key in his hand he left slowly prouder than ever because he had finally found all the answers he sought over all his life!!!

The End

To the people that got to know me during my lifetime
I dedicate this book to you
For you to find what you are looking for
For you to live your life truthfully
For you to find the purest form of love
I hope this book will inspire you
Sending my blessings

Paola Zanoni